at the beach
explore & discover
the New Zealand
seashore

Ned Barraud & Gillian Candler

craig potton publishing

For Rory, Leila & Alfie — NB
For Tobias — GC

Ned Barraud is a talented illustrator with a passion for sea creatures. His work has been published frequently in the *School Journal*, and he illustrated *The Earthquake and the Butterfly* (2012). He works at Weta Digital as a texture artist and lives in Wellington, spending lots of time exploring the seashore with his three young children.

Gillian Candler was a teacher for many years before moving into educational publishing with Learning Media in Wellington, where she worked as an editor, project manager and eventually CEO. She currently works as a writer and consultant from her home in Pukerua Bay, where she explores the beach most days.

Acknowledgements: Thanks to Rod Asher, Cawthron Institute, and Dr Don Morrisey, NIWA, for their expert review of text and illustrations.

First published in 2012 by Craig Potton Publishing

Craig Potton Publishing
98 Vickerman Street, PO Box 555, Nelson,
New Zealand
www.craigpotton.co.nz

Illustrations © Ned Barraud; text © Gillian Candler

ISBN PB 978-1-877517-73-0; HB 978-1-877517-74-7
Designed by Sarah Elworthy
Printed in China by Everbest Printing Co Ltd

staying safe at the beach

- stay close to adults
- keep off rocks if the weather is stormy or the sea is rough
- learn to swim

look after the beach & its creatures

- use a bucket with sea water in it to look at creatures, then put them back in the rock pools
- follow the rules about taking seafood
- don't leave rubbish at the beach
- take photos, not living things
- use binoculars to look at birds and sea mammals

contents

At the edge of the land where the sea begins, there are
sandy beaches, mudflats & rocky shores.

It's low tide. The beach is wide, the mudflats are exposed,
and the rock pools are nearly empty.

As the tide comes in, the salty sea water will creep up over
the mudflats and fill the rock pools, and the waves
will break high up on the beach.

Many animals and plants make their home at the beach.
They live in the sand and mud, or hang on tight to rocks.
Some even live underwater.

The creatures here have to watch out for other hungry
animals looking for a meal. Some dig into the sand to escape.
Some hide under rocks. Others have clever ways of protecting themselves.

Look carefully, as you turn the pages of this book,
to discover the plants and animals that live at the beach.

sandy beaches

Above the beach, dry sand is blown by the wind into sand dunes.
Grasses and other plants hold the sand in place with their roots.
Insects and birds live here too, above the reach of the sea.

When the tide goes out again, the sea leaves behind
driftwood, seaweed and sometimes pieces of sponge.

There are shells of all shapes and sizes
that were once home to many different
animals. Look at pages 20-23
to find out what they are.

6

If you look closely, you can see holes in the wet sand. Something is hiding there. Birds such as oystercatchers know this. They search for food, leaving their footprints behind in the wet sand.

ou may be lucky enough to see a crab shell r a glistening jellyfish near the water's dge, or some little fish arting around in the hallow water.

7

PAGE 30 *Black-backed gulls* are scavengers. They eat anything they can find.

Some *seaweeds* look like strings of beads. Others look like ribbons or lace. Some are dried and crunchy. Others are wet and slimy. PAGE 26

Holes in the sand are signs that shellfish are hiding. PAGE 22

Tiny *sandhoppers* feast on left-behind seaweed. PAGE 27

PAGE 30 *Oystercatchers* use their beaks to reach shellfish in the sand.

what lives on sandy beaches?

Sand is tiny pieces of rock ground up by the sea. Different kinds of rocks make different-coloured sand.

The *ostrich foot* feeds and breathes through tubes in holes in the sand. PAGE 22

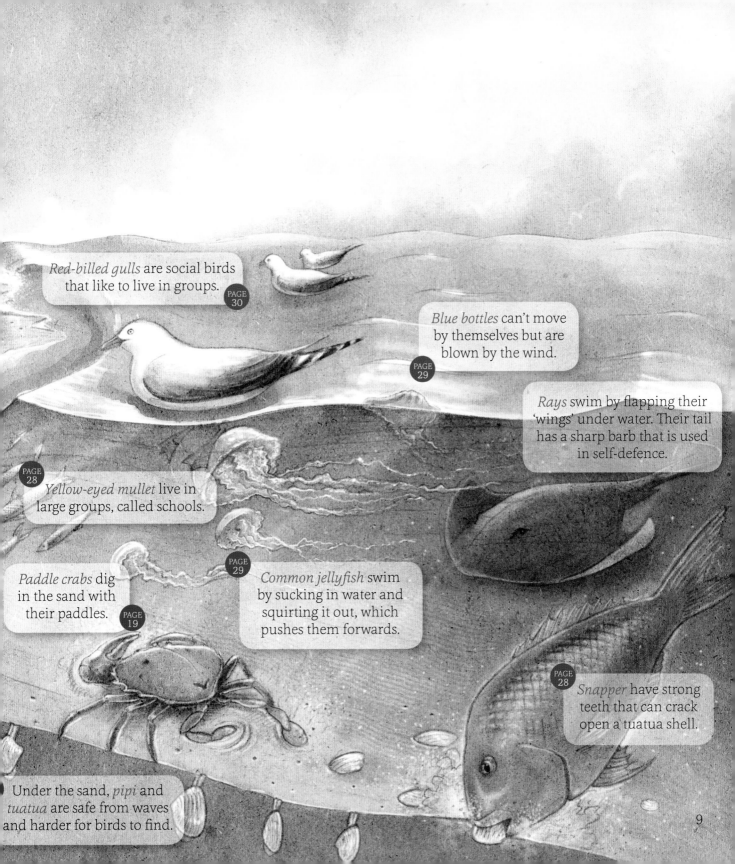

Red-billed gulls are social birds that like to live in groups. **PAGE 30**

Blue bottles can't move by themselves but are blown by the wind. **PAGE 29**

Rays swim by flapping their 'wings' under water. Their tail has a sharp barb that is used in self-defence.

PAGE 28 Yellow-eyed mullet live in large groups, called schools.

Paddle crabs dig in the sand with their paddles. **PAGE 19**

PAGE 29 Common jellyfish swim by sucking in water and squirting it out, which pushes them forwards.

PAGE 28 Snapper have strong teeth that can crack open a tuatua shell.

Under the sand, *pipi* and *tuatua* are safe from waves and harder for birds to find.

9

mudflats

Mudflats are made of mud that has been washed down from mountains and farms by slow-moving rivers and creeks. The mud settles and spreads out in estuaries, the places where the river or creek meets the sea.

At low tide, the only water is in small channels, which cross the mudflats like silver ribbons.

Mangroves grow in some estuaries, and their special breathing roots poke out of the mud.

Holes in the mud are signs that mud crabs and cockles are hiding. People dig for cockles in estuaries. Pied stilts and herons search for food too.

At high tide, the fresh water from the river mixes with the salty water from the sea and covers the mud flats.

what lives on mudflats?

Mangroves grow in the top part of the North Island. They have special roots so they can live in salty water. Fish and other small animals hide among the mangrove roots.

Mud crabs make burrows in the mud. These are safe places to hide when the tide goes out.

PAGE
18

Sea lettuce is eaten by crabs and fish.

PAGE
26

Cockles live in large groups called beds. They take in water through their feeding tubes and filter out tiny pieces of food.

PAGE
23

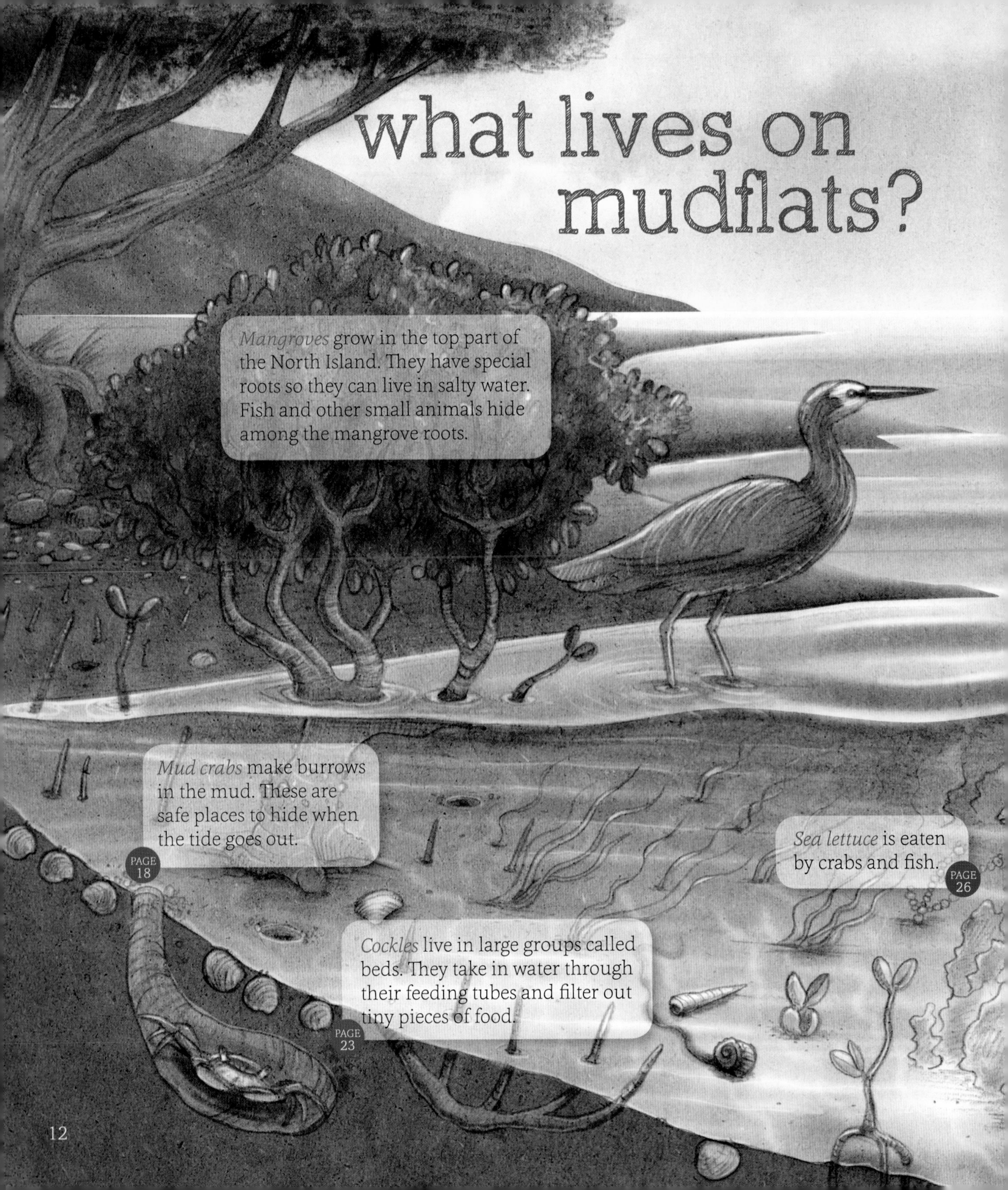

Pied stilts wade in the water with their long legs and search for food with their long beaks.
PAGE 31

Ducks can live in fresh water and salty water.
PAGE 31

Kingfishers dive into the water to catch a meal of yellow-eyed mullet.
PAGE 31

Flounder are camouflaged to look like the mud in the estuary.
PAGE 29

Mud snails eat mud and leave a trail of mud waste behind them.
PAGE 22

13

rocky shores

Many different animals live on the rocky shore.
There are lots of places for them to hide or find
shelter, as well as plenty for them to eat.

When it's high tide, the sea covers the rocks, filling up the rock pools. Fish and other animals swim and move around, looking for food.

Low tide is the best time to explore rock pools. You can see creatures like sea stars, kina and sea anemones. Sometimes shrimps and fish will be trapped in the shallow pools.

Seaweeds are fastened tightly to the rocks. So are barnacles and limpets, which can survive out of water for a long time.

Birds are looking in the rock pools for crabs and fish to eat, but crabs are hiding or using camouflage to escape the sharp beaks.

PAGE 30 The *pied shag* is drying its wings.

what lives on rocky shores?

PAGE 31 The *white-faced heron* has caught a crab.

Barnacles and *periwinkles* live at the high-tide line. PAGE 21

Neptune's necklace and *kelp* need sunlight to grow. PAGE 26

Cushion stars are scavengers and will eat anything they can find. PAGE 25

Chitons and *limpets* graze on algae and seaweed. They hold on tight to rocks so they are not washed away by waves and currents. PAGE 23

Sea anemones use their tentacles to catch tiny animals. They close up when the tide is low and there is no water to cover them. PAGE 25

The *hermit crab* has found a shell to live in. PAGE 18

This *black-backed gull* is dropping a mussel onto the rocks to break it open.

PAGE 30

Mussels filter the water to catch tiny particles to eat.

PAGE 23

Kina have spines, which make it harder for other animals to eat them.

PAGE 25

Shrimps are hard to see when they are not moving.

PAGE 29

Pāua have a black foot, which they use to move around on the rocks.

PAGE 22

Cockabullies can bury themselves in the sand to hide.

PAGE 28

Reef stars surround and hold their prey with the sucker-like feet on their arms.

PAGE 24

crabs

mud crab
kairau

Mud crabs are the colour of mud, which makes it easy for them to hide. They eat seaweed and plant material.

3 cm

kaunga waerau
hermit crab

Hermit crabs don't have a hard carapace like other crabs, so they look for an empty shell to live in. When they grow, they move into a bigger shell.

3 cm

half crab
kawekawe

You might think that half crabs have lost some legs but they grow this way. They hide under rocks or between stones and eat by filtering out tiny pieces of food from the water.

2 cm

shore crab or purple rock crab
pāpaka nui

Purple rock crabs live in rock pools. They hide under rocks during the day and scuttle around looking for food at night.

4 cm

camouflage crab
pāpaka huna

Camouflage crabs have a clever way of hiding in the rock pools. They use their claws to stick seaweed and sponges on to their shells so they look like rocks.

2 cm

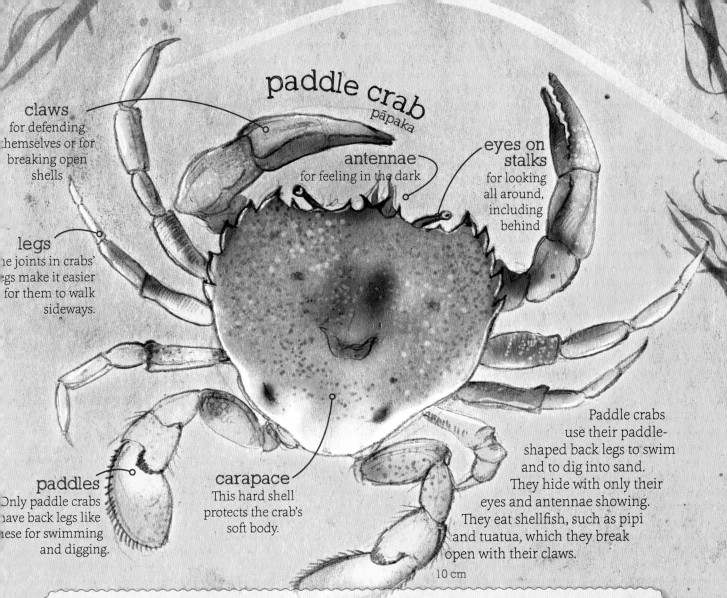

paddle crab
pāpaka

claws
for defending themselves or for breaking open shells

antennae
for feeling in the dark

eyes on stalks
for looking all around, including behind

legs
The joints in crabs' legs make it easier for them to walk sideways.

paddles
Only paddle crabs have back legs like these for swimming and digging.

carapace
This hard shell protects the crab's soft body.

Paddle crabs use their paddle-shaped back legs to swim and to dig into sand. They hide with only their eyes and antennae showing. They eat shellfish, such as pipi and tuatua, which they break open with their claws.

10 cm

crab facts

- Most crabs have *8 walking legs,* plus 2 that they use as claws.
- The fastest way for crabs to move is *sideways*.
- Crabs can *breathe under water* as well as out of the water.
- When a crab grows too big for its shell, it discards it and a new one grows in its place. This is called *moulting*. If you find an empty crab shell on the beach, it might be one that a crab has grown out of, not a dead crab.

- If a crab loses a leg, *it grows back again after it has moulted*.
- Most crabs are *scavengers*. They eat any food they can find, including dead animals and bits of seaweed.
- Crabs have clever ways of *hiding from predators*, which are other animals that like to eat them. Their main predators are birds and large fish.
- If you find a crab *under a rock*, make sure you put the rock back so it has somewhere to hide.

ostrich foot totorere 8 cm

triangle shell kaikaikaroro 7 cm

tuatua 8 cm

cockle tuangi 4 cm

pipi 6 cm

pāua 16 cm

mud snail whētiko 2 cm

whelk kawari 4 cm

mussel toretore 12

shells you might find on the beach

barnacles

pāitotito 1 cm

limpet

ngākihi 5 cm

cat's eye snail ata ata 7 cm

cat's eye

Cook's turban pūpū karikawa 9 cm

periwinkle

ngaeti 1 cm

Arabic volute pūpū rore

papatai
turret shell 8 cm

Pacific rock oyster

tio repe 8 cm

12 cm

scallop tipa 15 cm

ram's horn 2 cm

These shells were once part of living animals.
Turn the page to find out more about these animals.

shellfish

some have one shell, which may look like a snail shell

The animals that live inside are usually soft and the shell protects them from predators. They all have one large foot, which they use to move along, rather like the snails you find in your garden.

the ostrich foot and Arabic volute bury themselves in sand.

They breathe through tubes. The tubes make the holes that you see on the beach.

feeding tube

breathing tube

the turret shell and mud snail crawl on mud

They go inside their shell to protect themselves.

other shellfish live on rocks

Many of them graze on algae and seaweed that live on the rocks.

Whelks eat dying or dead animals and can smell their food from a long distance.

Cat's eye snails close their cat's eye (called an operculum) to protect themselves.

breathing hole

others have two shells joined with a hinge

These are called bivalves ('bi' means two). They open the shells to feed. The rings on the shells show how old they are. More rings means the shellfish is older.

blue mussels hold on to rocks with tough threads near their hinge

They filter food from water through feeding tubes.

pipi, cockles, tuatua and triangle shells bury themselves in sand or mud

They use their foot to dig into the sand, and breathe and feed through tubes.

hinge

foot
or burying
to the sand

scallops live out at sea

They swim by taking in water then squirting it out, which pushes them along. Scallops have one curved shell and one flat shell.

barnacles and chitons are made up of many separate parts

The shell-like plates of barnacles open for feeding when the tide is in and close when it goes out. They can live on other shells, rocks, boats and even whales.

The parts of chiton shells move separately, which makes it easy for them to bend and squeeze into narrow gaps.

when is a shell not a shell? ram's horn

Ram's horn shells that you find on the beach are not shellfish at all but come from inside a squid.

23

sea stars, kina &
sea anemones

suckers
are on the underside of the arms and help sea stars move around and hold onto rocks.

reef star

pātangaroa
Reef stars are large sea stars that like to eat mussels and kina. They usually have 10 to 12 arms.

25 cm

spines
on top of the arms protect the reef star.

mouth
This is underneath the centre of the animal. When sea stars eat, they push their stomach out through their mouth and on to their food. Their stomach then digests the food.

sea star facts

- These animals are often called star fish but, as *they are not fish*, some scientists prefer to call them sea stars.

- There are *many different kinds of sea stars* and each kind can be many *different colours*, such as blue, red, orange or green.

- They don't have eyes but *can detect light and dark* through the tips of their arms.

- If you see a sea star with arms of different lengths, it has *split itself in half* to make two new sea stars and is growing some new arms.

- If a sea star loses a leg, *it can grow a new one*.

cushion star

kapu parahua

Cushion stars are small sea stars that have 4 to 6 arms. They are scavengers and will eat small animals, such as barnacles.

6 cm

sea anemone

stinging tentacles

kōtore moana

These sea anemones like to live on rocks where there is no sun or wind. They close up when the tide goes out and open again when they are covered by water. They move by sliding along the rock.

open

closed

2 cm

wandering sea anemone

kōtore moana

Wandering sea anemones float in the water but can also hold onto rocks or kelp to stay in one place. The best time to see them is at night, when they move around looking for food.

20 cm

sea anemone facts

- Sea anemones look like plants but are actually *animals*.
- They use *stinging tentacles* to catch tiny fish and shrimps.
- They can be many *different colours*.
- If you touch the tentacles of a sea anemone, it will quickly *close up* to protect itself.

Kina eat seaweed, such as kelp. They are eaten by fish and sea stars, and people like to eat them too. Between their spines are long tube feet.

kina

sea urchin

10 cm

spines for protection and trapping food

shell of dead kina

kina facts

- The *mouth* of the kina is underneath.
- The *shell of a dead kina* looks quite different without the spines and feet.

tube feet for moving around and holding onto rocks

live kina

25

seaweeds, sponges & sandhoppers

Neptune's necklace

This seaweed lives in rock pools. The bobbles are full of water, so it doesn't dry out when it's out of the water.

sea lettuce

Sea lettuce is bright green. It grows in shallow water in mudflats and estuaries.

common kelp

Kelp grows in underwater forests and is often found washed up on the beach. It bends easily so it can move in the water. Other kinds of kelp are bull kelp and bladder kelp.

holdfast
for gripping tightly onto rocks or the sea floor

finger sponge

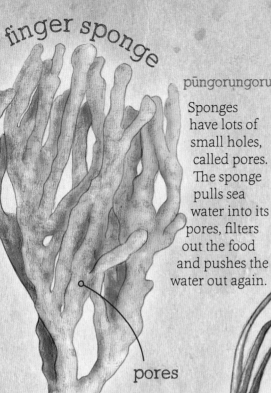

pūngorungoru

Sponges have lots of small holes, called pores. The sponge pulls sea water into its pores, filters out the food and pushes the water out again.

pores

sponge facts

- Sponges look like plants but are actually *animals*.
- They can be many *different shapes and colours*. Some look like orange balls.
- Sponges can *live for 50 years* or more.
- Some fish *eat sponges*.

bladder kelp

Bladder kelp grows very fast, up to 50 cm a day. Bladders of air help it to float.

sandhopper facts

- Sandhoppers are *crustaceans*, like shrimps and crabs.
- They are *eaten by birds and fish*.
- Sandhoppers can *jump* up to 30 cm.

sandhopper

mōwhitiwhiti

Sandhoppers hide in and eat dead seaweed that has been washed up on the beach.

1 cm

seaweed facts

- The Māori name for seaweed is *rimurimu*.
- Seaweed *needs light* from the sun to grow.
- Seaweed can be *pink, red, green or brown*.
- The *pink covering* you sometimes see on rocks is a kind of seaweed called coralline turf. Cat's eye snails and other shellfish graze on this.
- Seaweed is eaten by many creatures, including pāua, kina, crabs and fish.
- Seaweed is used in many of the *foods we eat*, like yoghurt and ice cream. It contains lots of vitamins.

27

fish, jellyfish & shrimps

Cockabully is the name for ma
different, tiny rock-pool fi
They hide between the rocks a
in seaweed, and they can a
bury themselves in sa

snapper tāmure

fins
keep fish upright and help
them move through
the water.

scales
Many fish have slippery,
shiny scales instead of skin,
but rays and sharks have
a thick, leathery skin.

Snapper
have strong
teeth. They eat crabs,
kina and shellfish.

50 cm

gills
for breathing
under water

yellow-eyed mullet 30 cm

aua

These fish live
in shallow waters at
the beach, in harbours, mudflats
and around mangroves. They eat algae and
small animals. Predators are larger fish, and
birds such as herons and kingfishers.

fish facts

- There are more than *1000 different kinds* of fish in the seas around New Zealand.

- Fish *can't live out of water*. Their gills are designed for breathing underwater.

- When fish jump out of the water, it may be because they are being *chased by other larger fish* looking for a meal.

- *Rays* are the largest fish you might see close to the shore. They can grow to 2 or 3 metres wide.

10 cm

ihumoana
blue bottle

These are not real jellyfish. They are a group of tiny animals living under a floating blue air bag. Don't touch dead blue bottles on the beach because their tentacles sting, even when they are dead.

5 cm

jellyfish facts

- Jellyfish are *not fish*. They are also called jellies or sea jellies.
- They *move* by sucking in water then squirting it out, which pushes them forwards.
- Most jelllyfish give a very painful *sting* if you touch them.
- Fish and whales *eat jellyfish*. Sometimes they eat plastic bags by mistake, thinking they are jellyfish.

common jellyfish

flounder
pātiki
45 cm

Baby flounder look like other fish, but as they grow, one of their eyes moves until both eyes are on the same side. Flounder eat cockles and crabs.

petipeti

This jellyfish eats tiny animals, which it catches with its stinging tentacles. Its sting doesn't hurt people.

20 cm

stinging tentacles

shrimp facts

- Shrimps are *crustaceans*, like crabs and sandhoppers.
- They *eat tiny animals and plants* in the rock pool.
- They have *10 legs*.

antennae

shrimp
2 cm

kōura rangi

It can be hard to spot shrimps in a rock pool because they are small and transparent (you can almost see through them.) Shrimps use their long antennae to feel for food.

29

black-backed gull

karoro

These gulls eat shellfish, such as mussels and tuatua. They are also scavengers and will eat your picnic food or dead fish that are washed up on the beach. Gulls nest on rocky cliffs.

60 cm

adult gull

young gull

Oystercatchers use their long, orange beaks to reach down into the sand. Their beaks are strong enough to break open shells. They make their nests in the sand or among stones on the beach.

red-billed gull

akiaki

Red-b gulls smalle than bla backed gul

37 cm

oystercatcher

tōrea

45 cm

pied shag

kāruhiruhi

Shags dive for fish, sometimes staying under water for 20 seconds. Once they are back on land, they hold their wings out to dry. Shags make nests in trees on the coast.

80 cm

birds

white-fronted tern

tara

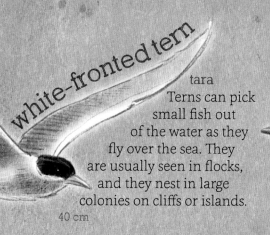

Terns can pick small fish out of the water as they fly over the sea. They are usually seen in flocks, and they nest in large colonies on cliffs or islands.

40 cm

kingfisher

kōtare

Kingfishers sit up high on rocks, trees or wires looking out for food. They eat fish, crabs, insects and other animals. Kingfishers have very good eyesight but can't move their eyes so they move their head to watch their prey.

24 cm

white-faced heron

matuku moana

These birds stand very still so that crabs and fish can't see them. Then they dart very quickly to catch their prey with their sharp beak.

65 cm

bird facts

- Some birds, such as gulls and terns, live in large groups called *flocks or colonies*. Others, like kingfishers, *live alone*, in pairs, or in family groups.

- Birds have different-shaped *beaks* to get the food they like. Bill is another word for beak.

- Most birds *sleep at night*, so other animals are safe from these predators after dark.

- A good way to learn more about birds at the beach is to watch them through *binoculars*.

pied stilt

poaka

Pied stilts are wading birds that like mudflats, harbours and rivers. Their long legs mean they can stand in water to look for shellfish, which they catch with their long beak.

35 cm

duck

rakiraki

Ducks mostly live on fresh-water lakes and rivers, but they also like harbours and estuaries. Ducks have wide, flat beaks that are good for finding things to eat in the mud, such as worms or shellfish.

55 cm

glossary

algae A group of plant-like living things that includes seaweeds. Algae can also be very small.

antennae Body parts used for feeling in the dark.

beds Places where groups of shellfish live together in the sand.

bivalve A shellfish that has two shells joined together by a hinge.

camouflage Skin or covering that matches an animal's surroundings so that the animal is hard to see.

carapace The name for the hard shell on the outside of a crab.

colonies Large groups of birds or other animals that live together.

estuary Where a river or creek meets the sea. Fresh water from the river mixes with salty water from the sea.

filter To get tiny pieces of food out of water.

fresh water Water from lakes, rivers and rain.

graze To use teeth or mouth parts to chew or scrape algae off rocks.

moult To get rid of a body covering and grow a new one, like a crab gets rid of its shell.

mudflat A wide, open space of mud and fine sand deposited by tides and river water.

predator An animal that hunts and eats other animals.

scavenger An animal that eats anything it can find, including animals that are already dead.

school A group of fish.

sea water Sea water contains a lot of salt. Creatures that live in the sea are used to this but it is too salty for people and other animals that live on land and are used to fresh water.

tentacle A long flexible body part used for feeling, grasping or stinging.

tide The tide is the changing height of the water at the beach. Every day there are two low tides and two high tides. The times of these change slightly every day.

index

find out more

Visit a marine reserve or aquarium, check out books from your local library, or go to these websites:

Information about New Zealand animals, plants & seaweeds
www.teara.govt.nz Te Ara—The Encyclopedia of New Zealand
www.marine.ac.nz New Zealand Marine Studies Centre, University of Otago
www.kcc.org.nz Kiwi Conservation Club

Fishing rules & limits
www.fish.govt.nz Ministry of Fisheries

Marine Reserves
www.doc.govt.nz Department of Conservation

Tide times & weather conditions
www.metservice.com Met Service

Information for parents & teachers about this book
www.craigpotton.co.nz/at-the-beach